ALL ABOUT MEDIA

KT-560-414

STAY SAFE ONLINE

BRIEN J JENNINGS

Raintree is an imprint of Capstone Global Library Limited, a company incorporated in England and Wales having its registered office at 264 Banbury Road, Oxford, OX2 7DY – Registered company number: 6695582

www.raintree.co.uk
myorders@raintree.co.uk

Text © Capstone Global Library Limited 2018
The moral rights of the proprietor have been asserted.

Printed and bound in India

ISBN 978 1 4747 5438 5 (hardback)
22 21 20 19 18
10 9 8 7 6 5 4 3 2 1

ISBN 978 1 4747 5442 2 (paperback)
23 22 21 20 19
10 9 8 7 6 5 4 3 2 1

Editorial credits:
Erika L. Shores, editor; Juliette Peters, designer;
Morgan Walters, media researcher; Kathy McColley, production specialist

Photo credits:
Alamy: Mamunur Rashid, 5; Capstone Studio: Karon Dubke, Cover; Shutterstock: Africa Studio, 17, Artur. B, (icons) design element, Daisy Daisy, 15, Kaspri, 10, LightField Studios, 9, Monkey Business Images, 7, Supphachai Salaeman, design element throughout, Uber Images, 13, vectorfusionart, 11, wavebreakmedia, 19, 21, Wright Studio, 6, 20

British Library Cataloguing in Publication Data
A full catalogue record for this book is available from the British Library.

Contents

Being online 4
Privacy matters 6
Staying safe 10
Cyberbullying 14
Be a good digital citizen 18

Glossary. 22
Books 23
Websites 23
Comprehension questions 24
Index. 24

Being online

How hot is the sun? How is your pen pal? If you want to know the answer to either question, you may decide to go **online**. In the past, people had to go to the library or write a letter to find out the answers to these questions.

The internet is a great tool. People use it to play games and shop. People all over the world use the internet to communicate with each other. But, as with any tool, you need to be safe when using the internet.

---

online connected to the internet

Fact! The internet is a network of computers. Underground cables that stretch around the world connect the computers.

Privacy matters

The internet allows you to connect with other people. But it also allows other people to connect with you – even strangers. That's not always a good thing. When you're online, it's important to protect your private information.

Remembering important rules will help keep you safe online. Always ask a **trusted adult** before downloading applications or setting up **accounts** on game websites or **social media**. Ask for help finding and using the privacy settings on these programs. Don't allow friends to tag you in photos on social media. If you are tagged in a photo, ask an adult to help you remove it.

Tip! When you need a **password**, make it as hard to guess as possible. You don't want anyone to know it. Do not use passwords such as 123456, 12345678 and "password". They are too easy for another person to guess.

trusted adult grown-up who you know well, who is honest and reliable

account arrangement by which a user is given personal access to a computer, website or application, typically by entering a username and password

social media websites that allow people to share words, pictures and videos with other people

Staying safe

Staying safe starts with knowing what not to share. While online, do not give out your age or full name. Instead, you should make up a **screen name**, or username. You should never share your home address or school name. Keep information about family members, and where they work, private. Never share pictures with strangers.

screen name made-up name that a
person uses when he or she is online

11

Why would anyone want someone's private information? Often people may want to sell the information to companies. Companies use this information to get more customers. Other reasons are more harmful. Some people may want to put **viruses** on a computer or take control of it. Others may want to bully someone with mean messages and spread lies.

---

virus program that copies itself and can harm computers and other digital devices

Think about it!

Be careful about how much you share. Think twice before you post a message or a photo. It's possible for strangers to see what you put online. Always tell a trusted adult if something you see online makes you uncomfortable.

Cyberbullying

Bullies can be found at school and on the internet. Cyberbullies are people who post mean and hurtful messages about others online. Cyberbullies can be people you do not know. But they can also be people you know from school or other activities. You could also be a bully even though you may not mean to be hurtful. Think before you send or share comments or pictures.

Bullies can be hard to avoid. This is true for cyberbullies too. But there are some ways to deal with them. If someone is posting or sharing mean things or lies, don't respond. Block them if it's possible. Always show mean posts to a trusted adult.

Be a good digital citizen

Everyone who uses the internet needs to be respectful and polite. Think twice before sharing information, pictures or stories. They may not be true. Don't pretend to be someone else – even if it's a joke, it can be harmful.

> **FACT!** Things you post and share online may still be there even after you delete them.

Using the internet is a big **responsibility**. Being a good digital citizen means thinking about keeping yourself and others safe. Start simple habits such as reporting cyberbullies and keeping personal information private. It will help everyone stay safe online.

responsibility
duty or job

Glossary

account arrangement by which a user is given personal access to a computer, website or application, typically by entering a username and password

online connected to the internet

password secret code usually made up of a combination of letters, words or numbers

responsibility duty or job

screen name made-up name that a person uses when he or she is online

social media websites that allow people to share words, pictures and videos with other people

trusted adult grown-up who you know well, who is honest and reliable

virus program that copies itself and can harm computers and other digital devices

Books

Let's Think About the Internet and Social Media (Let's Think About), Alex Woolf (Raintree, 2015)

Sometimes Jokes Aren't Funny: What to do about hidden bullying (No More Bullies), Melissa Higgins (Raintree, 2016)

Staying Safe Online (Our Digital Planet), Ben Hubbard (Raintree, 2017)

Websites

www.bbc.co.uk/cbbc/shows/stay-safe
Follow this guide to staying safe on the internet.

www.dkfindout.com/uk/computer-coding/what-is-internet/
Find out more about how the internet works.

Comprehension questions

1. What can you do to stay safe online?

2. Is cyberbullying more than just being mean? Why?

3. List some of the personal information you should never share online.

Index

accounts 8

applications (apps) 8

computers 5

cyberbullies 12, 14, 16, 20

digital citizens 20

games 4, 8

libraries 4

media 4

passwords 8

posting 13, 18

privacy 6, 10, 12, 20

privacy settings 8

research 4

screen names 10

social media 8

strangers 6, 10, 13

trusted adults 8, 13, 16

usernames 10

viruses 12